ONE WAY
to where?

A Regal Jesus Person Maturity Book
by David Wilkerson

The truth about the drug
habit ... how it begins, seldom
discussed effects, clarification of
contradictory evidence and facts,
and what God has to say about a
cure.

D1115348

Regal Books:
A Division of G/L Publications
Glendale, California, U.S.A.

This book is made up of portions of
Jesus Person Maturity Manual and
Jesus Person Pocket Promise Book.

Dan Peters: Design
Illustrations: Preston Heiselt

Photography:

Gary Conniff—pages 4,15,22,26,28,30,33,40,43,45,48,50,53.
Bob Combs—pages 6,9,12,18,20,54.
Ron Widman—pages 14,34,46.

Scripture quoted from:

Authorized Version (KJV)
New American Standard Bible, © The Lockman Foundation, 1971.
Used by permission.

The Living Bible, Paraphrased (Wheaton: Tyndale House Publishers, 1971).
Used by permission.

Printed in U.S.A.

Published by
Regal Books Division, G/L Publications
Glendale, California 91209, U.S.A.

Library of Congress Catalog No. 72-83847
ISBN 0-8307-0169-9

Contents

pot

I used to be a traveling crusader against pot. I had a briefcase full of stories and information about how it leads to hard stuff, especially heroin. I appeared on shows with Merv Griffin, Mike Douglas, Virginia Graham, Art Linkletter and others warning students about the dangers of blowing "smoke."

But I have been converted. Not that I think that marijuana is any less harmful than it was before. I still consider it very dangerous. But all the scare tactics, all the education, all the lecturing, is absolutely in vain for those who have already made up their minds to turn on with pot.

The great marijuana debate will continue long after all the research has ended. When the statistics are tabulated and the findings of doctors and research agencies are made public, the use of pot will still not diminish. The horrifying commercials on TV against tobacco smoking

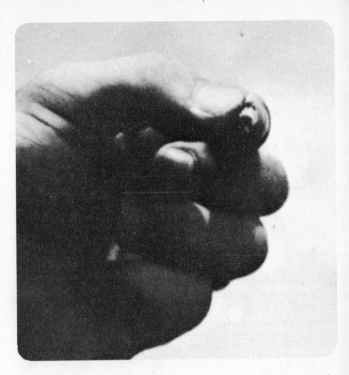

scared a lot of people, but kids are still starting to smoke at a fast pace. Not a single tobacco company is going out of business. Likewise, an avalanche of facts will not turn a single student away from pot or acid once he is committed to this course.

Those who smoke pot defend it vociferously. They know all the angles and can reel off all the arguments. They read up on the subject and become "pot conscious." They look down on anybody who speaks out against it, suggesting they are misinformed, uncool, or just too square. They choose to ignore any fact or philosophy that runs afoul of their ideas about pot.

When I lectured on campus about the dangers of pot, I was swamped with all the arguments prevalent for the rationalizing of pot smoking.....

Drug abusers seem to need every excuse they can find. Perhaps this explains the reason why most of the books defending the use of drugs are written by admitted drug users.

If it is not as harmful as once believed, why all the fuss about its use? Not enough penetrating research has been conducted regarding marijuana and very little is yet known of its long-term effects. Current research will give us the answers to many questions in the near future. However, it will be 25 years before we know the long-range effects. We may yet learn that marijuana causes cancer, as do cigarettes. Also, there may be slow but permanent brain cell damage. At one time doctors said morphine was less harmless than alcohol. That was before research proved its dangerous addicting power.

Marijuana may not be addictive but it is for many psychologically habituating, causing a dependence or a need in times of emotional conflict. It becomes a way of escape. In its strongest forms, marijuana can cause psychotic reactions in almost anyone. Marijuana causes a distortion in concepts of time, space and distance.

I say marijuana is dangerous because few people recognize the true dangers. Kids say, ''I know it can't hurt me—I have read all about it and it's harmless.'' The trouble is they believe only the sources of information with which they agree and refuse to accept information given by recognized experts who speak out on the medical dangers of marijuana. I have worked with large numbers of teenagers who were psychologically dependent upon marijuana.

The breakdown of inhibitions is one of the main reasons kids like to smoke pot. If their trip is not a "bummer," they "go up" to a false sense of confidence, power and ability. Pot can cause paranoid feelings, depression and apprehension. The user often experiences phantasmagoria, the sensation that figures are rushing toward him at tremendous speed, increasing in size as they approach, and decreasing in size as they leave—similar to a zoom lens on a camera. The effects are short-lived but often so intense that this disorientation leads to temporary psychosis.

Marijuana joints burn hotter than regular cigarettes and the fumes are held in the lungs and exhaled slowly. Adequate long-range research may yet confirm definite lung damage. Potency of marijuana varies from batch to batch and therein lies the unknown danger. For example, Vietnam-type marijuana is so potent that when mixed with oregano or dehydrated horse manure, as is often the case, anything can happen!

People who get stoned on alcohol or high on marijuana and drive like maniacs on our highways are equally dangerous. Last year alcohol caused, directly or indirectly, more than 5 million psychotic disorders. It is foolish to justify the adoption of one vice (marijuana) by trying to prove it is no worse than existing vices, alcohol or tobacco. There is a terrible double standard in the country today. Some experts write pamphlets warning kids to stay away from pot and then go home to a bottle of Scotch.

The best experts in the world do not confirm marijuana is harmless. It all depends on which "experts" you are listening to. The experts who research for *Playboy* magazine dispute the research done by the Federal Bureau of Narcotics. I have studied the findings of experts all over the world and have been surprised by the double talk and childish rationalization by some. Joel Fort, M.D.,

who claims to have studied drug laws in 30 nations and researched drugs for 15 years, calls for the legalization of marijuana because he claims it is absolutely harmless. He recommends, as do some other experts, that marijuana be produced under federal supervision, the sellers be licensed, and sales made only to those over 18. But—get this—he wants the marijuana packages to carry the following warning:

CAUTION: Marijuana may be harmful to your health.

If marijuana is harmless, why carry a warning? I call this double talk! The majority of legitimate experts agree with Dr. Herbert A. Roskin, clinical associate professor of psychiatry at Wayne State University, ". . .We're also beginning to see cases in which a marijuana high comes on again spontaneously, weeks after the person has had a high. . . . We've also had some young people with acute psychosis brought on by marijuana."

I'VE TRIED POT AND IT NEVER AFFECTED ME ADVERSELY. MY FRIENDS TURN ON AND THEY'VE NEVER HAD A BAD EXPERIENCE, EITHER.

Legions of people who smoke pot say the penalties against the sale and use of marijuana are still too stiff and that all the restrictions are discriminatory; they want it legalized. These are not just hippies and drop-outs, but some are Wall Street brokers, engineers, poverty workers, government officials, professionals, and others in various walks of life. The truth is, there are some 1,600 drugs included under the drug-abuse law which cannot be taken legally without a prescription. The abuse of these drugs also carries a penalty.

The Real Truth About Pot

One joint may never hurt you. A thousand "tokes" may not get to you. You may drag on pot for a long time and never go on to junk or hard stuff. Pot was not invented in recent years, it is ancient. I had found pot being used freely when I started working with drug users in the ghetto twelve years ago. The only thing new about pot is its wide-spread misuse among middle class educated young people and its spread into "respectable" society. As long as it was the problem of the ghettos nobody seemed to bother. Now that pot is "in" with the affluent sons and daughters of the well known and respected, everybody is sounding the alarm.

There is no doubt about it—recent polls reveal that a large percentage of the kids who are on pot today are among the most intelligent and sophisticated in their class. There is not a single town in the country today that has not been affected. Complacent adults can quit sitting around waiting for pot to go out of style like the Hoola Hoop—pot is here to stay because it does exactly what youth wants it to do and exactly what adults do not want it to do. It polarizes and widens every gap.

But students themselves, quite apart from the scare tactics of the adult generation, are beginning to see that pot really is a nothing path to nowhere. One student put it like this:

"Smoking grass is really silly. You go through the ridiculous ritual of taking a toke, holding your breath, burning your throat, and getting red-eyed. You constantly worry about someone unexpectedly knocking on the door to enter the room."

I have personally worked with numbers of students habituated to pot. The experts keep telling me they are only psychologically habituated, not physiologically. But who cares about semantics, if the user can't get along without it, if it becomes a habit of the mind, he is still hooked and needs help.

Before I say another word, let me get one thing straight. I don't buy this idea going around that nearly every high school kid is a pot-head, that the majority of college

students are acid freaks. The drug abusers may take the headlines and put parents in a state of panic, but the truth of the matter is that the majority of students will continue to reject the drug route.

Street junkies think of pot as the beginning of the "route." One mainliner put it this way:

"If a junkie is lucky he will have a friend who will stand by him: but when the time comes, only he can make the decision to stay clean. Even then it's never easy. Along with the patterns of escape your mind has developed, you must fight your physiological craving. I would be satisfied if I could turn off just one kid who is thinking of doing junk."

It creeps up on you. It's all fun at first, a real groove. It could be the second joint or the two hundredth, but eventually you turn on to forget some problem, to feel good, to drift away from a situation that bothers you. Then friend, you are in real trouble because you are running. You will find it easier each time just to space out and not face reality. It's a cop-out! And the problems just won't go away.

Pot smokers resent the idea they are developing "patterns of escape." But those who have gone the whole route tell another story. Actor Joe Robinson, who played the role of Caesar in *The Robe*, turned to drugs at 23. He lost his movie contract and turned on with hard stuff. Now, after many tragic years, he is making a great comeback. Interviewed recently, Joey said:

"For those who say lighter drugs aren't harmful, I say they open the door to harder drugs. If you've tried one, why not another one, as I did? Once drug use begins, you gradually drop out of life."

The Jesus Person does not condemn others who blow pot, but refuses to indulge himself because he will not abuse the Temple of God, his body.

To the Jesus Person, all the arguments about pot are ridiculous. Why seek a phony high when the heart is already filled with joy and peace through Christ!

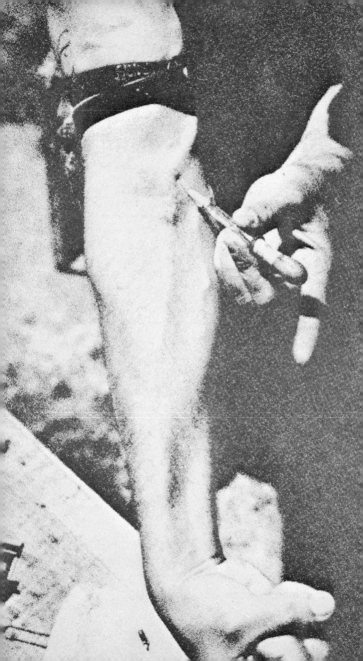

heroin

The heroin "route" begins with "sniffing" the stuff through the nostrils. Normally a "bag" of heroin (a small cellophane envelope) contains 200 milligrams of powder, just enough to cover a thumbnail. Of this, 15 to 30 milligrams can be heroin. The rest is "garbage"—quinine, milk sugar (lactose, maltose or glucose). The bag is held to the nostrils and the powder is "snorted" into the head passages. The second stage of heroin addiction is "skin popping"—diluting the powder with hot water and injected by needle into the upper arm. Users are preconvinced they will never get hooked if they stay away from hitting a vein. But the body becomes tolerant. The high gets thin and in desperation, the user begins "hitting" the main veins (called mainlining) and about 15 mainline hits and he is psychologically addicted for life. In 12 years of working with addicts, I find less than one in one hundred who were able to quit once they started using it in any way. It is a dead-end street to emptiness.

Heroin peddled by street corner pushers is dirty, often mixed with toxic agents such as rat poison, strychnine, and powder from car battery terminals. Even when a dose is weak, the added toxins can cause death due to bacterial infections caused by dirty needles. These include endocarditus (inflammation of heart valves), tetanus, and viral hepatitis. Methadone, a synthetic narcotic, is now supplied by narcotic addiction control centers to heroin addicts as a substitute. In New York City 10,000 addicts each year receive a regular supply of methadone. Heralded as

a "substitute," fantastic claims are being made that heroin users getting methadone have become productive members of their communities. But one form of addiction is substituted for another—he is still an addict—still dependent—still crippled—and still maintained by the state as a drug dependent for the rest of his life. We have personally dealt with many addicts who were on methadone, who are convinced it is not the answer—and does not help because the addict loses his desire to be cured.

Medically, there is not much chance for a cure. But, through programs specializing in spiritual as well as physical therapy, there is a tremendous cure rate. Less than 5% of the addicts treated in present medical facilities find a cure. It is primarily because the addict, who leaves the hospital physically clean and detoxicated, has no work record and no re-entry assistance, and is forced back into the hopeless cycle that led him into addiction. Teen Challenge is one of a number of successful drug treatment programs. Featuring "cold turkey" withdrawal and intense spiritual and vocational guidance, the addicts are led through various stages to complete freedom from narcotics—physically and psychologically.

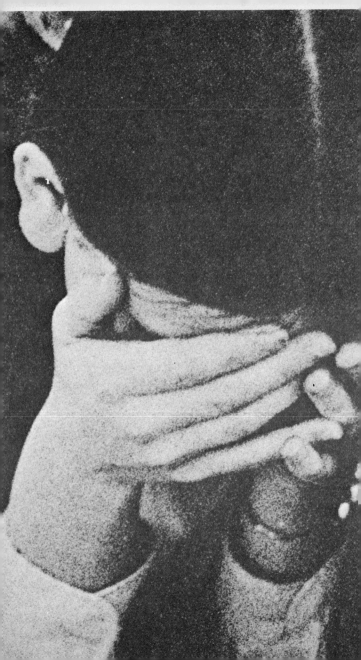

pills

Pills are amphetamines and barbiturates—sedatives and stimulants that affect the central nervous system.

Pills circulating today are mostly black market pills produced by illegal companies. Large shipments come in from Mexico, where it is possible for pharmacists to buy loads of pills and resell them in the black market. The Drug Abuse Control Amendments of 1965 require detailed records on the manufacture, shipment, and distribution of all stimulants, depressants and hallucinogens. The law declares a barbiturate or amphetamine prescription is good for only six months and during that time is limited to five refills. These prescriptions are often traced on stolen prescription pads and forged. These forged prescriptions are taken to various drug stores all over the city to avoid detection.

Three teenagers broke into a doctor's office in Detroit and stole three gallon bottles of dangerous pills. Somewhere in that city a group of foolish teenagers are playing a very dangerous game.

I can tell you, after working for twelve years with thousands of addicts, pill addiction is the worst kind. I have seen the madness, the terror—the horrible insanity—all brought on by pills. I have seen the razor-scarred arms and legs of people on pills who attempted suicide—many until they finally succeeded. I have buried them. I stand over the caskets of kids who once said, "Everybody's doing it—just be careful—it's not so dangerous."

There are many "silent abusers" today. They take pills in the privacy of their bedrooms and try not to disturb anyone in the home or community. Many are middle-aged people and older, those we never think of as addicts. Unable to face life and responsibility, they escape through "bottled emotions." A pill is taken to wake up—another to stay awake—another kind to sleep and one to forget everything. "Pill drunks" often stay bedridden in a complete stupor. When they are sober they are confused, irritable, uncoordinated and depressed. The body becomes tolerant and larger doses are needed, throwing the chemical balance out of control. People who go on an "amphetamine spree" may collapse from total exhaustion and damage the heart, causing death. Mental illness is the greatest hazard from "popping" pills. Amphetamine psychosis causes individuals to believe others are plotting to kill him, or he sees and hears things that aren't really there.

The use of pills causes strong physical dependence; in other words, pills hook you! Withdrawal is a life and death matter. "Cold turkey" (sudden withdrawal with no medication) could be fatal. Most pill addicts have to be hospitalized for withdrawal. Withdrawal from pills is accompanied by convulsions, delirium, delusions, cramps, flashbacks and excruciating body pains. Once you are "hooked" you cannot stop without help—and the cure rate is very low.

acid

Acid is lysergic acid diethylamide, an odorless, tasteless, colorless potent hallucinogenic drug.

LSD is a dangerous, unpredictable disaster drug. It is a chemical so powerful that an amount smaller than a grain of salt can "trip out" a person. A single ounce is enough to provide 300,000 average doses. This mind-bending drug is noted mainly for causing bizarre mental reactions and striking distortions in physical senses. Everything becomes fluid—every sense is affected. An average dose has an effect that lasts about 8 to 10 hours.

In 1943, scientists began to experiment with LSD in controlling schizophrenia, a mental disorder in which patients live in a fantasy world. Controlled research still goes on. Meanwhile, prominent people, authors, movie stars, magazine editors and public officials experimented with

this drug and gave glowing accounts of "beautiful" trips. Since then, LSD use has spread like cancer around the world. Curiosity seekers jumped on the bandwagon. Word was out that LSD helped create God consciousness—personal insights—heavenly visions—trips to the eternal—and could assist in solving difficult problems. Self-improvers, poets, musicians all hitched their wagons to this new "star" to help them be more creative, original and unique.

In short time the harvest came in! LSD intoxication triggered mental collapse nationwide. Murders, suicides, insanity, blindness, chromosomal breakage was discovered everywhere the drug was used. "Flashbacks" recur even six and ten months after taking LSD, and users experience horrifying hallucinations.

There is no evidence to prove any self-discovery. LSD users find that when the effect wears off, their friends don't recognize the "new image." They begin to believe a lie, supposing they are more perceptive and less ego conscious. They alter their personality, and won't accept the fact they are coming apart.

Black market LSD is contaminated with impurities ranging from 20% to 60%. The unknown substances and impurities in crude LSD make it hazardous and very dangerous. There are now more than 65 crude forms of psychedelics on the black market. STP (4-methyl 2, 5 dimethoxy-alpha methyl phenethylamine) is called sydicot acid. It can kill.

STP, speed, 68, LSD, 25, IT 290, and many other formulas are flooding the black market. These dirty syndicate drugs are soaked on ink blotters and sold in capsule and pill form, and are often made by students in school labs. Taking LSD under the strictest controlled situation is unpredictable and dangerous. Taking "dirty" acid in an LSD "crash" party can lead to death—NOW!

The Jesus Person refuses to drop acid because he has already found what he is looking for. The search ends in Jesus Christ. Acid is a phony trip taken only by those who cannot accept the claims of Christ who offers absolute peace and purpose in life.

a message to drug addicts only

Dear Drug Addict:

It's about time somebody told you the truth about your habit! You've been lying, cheating, stealing and working angles ever since you got hooked—now it's time to stop and do some hard thinking for just ten minutes. If you like the stuff and just want to control your habit—NO ONE CAN HELP YOU! Get this straight—THERE IS NO HOPE FOR YOU UNLESS YOU ARE DESPERATE FOR HELP! Take a good look at yourself! You thought you were different—you thought you would never get hooked. You thought you would never have to mug or break in—you never thought you'd end up like a beggar just living from one fix to another. You didn't want to admit you were getting hooked but now you can't fool yourself any longer. YOU'RE A JUNKIE—YOU'RE HOOKED—YOU'RE LOSING YOUR LIFE AND YOUR SOUL! If you like the kind of life you're living—don't read another word. I want to talk just to addicts who are sick of junk and who want to start a new life!

THERE IS A LIFETIME CURE FOR DRUG ADDICTION! It doesn't matter how long a run you have had—you can be cured. There are FIVE STEPS to this cure!

STEP NUMBER ONE: ADMIT YOU ARE HOOKED!

· It doesn't matter whether you take off once a day or ten times a day—you are hooked—so why not admit it?

· Quit talking about a big habit or a little habit. A habit is a habit—you're either hooked or you're not hooked—so be honest! If you don't think you're hooked now—just wait—it won't be long!

· Quit trying to cut it down yourself—you can't do it. You know you can't help yourself so why do you keep trying?

· No one can help you if you just want to control your habit or shoot it up on weekends. There is no such thing as a controlled habit. You will shoot all you can get and you know it.

· Admit to yourself: "I'm a drug addict! I'm hooked! I can't help myself!" Then you are ready for the next step.

STEP NUMBER TWO: QUIT LOOKING FOR AN EASY WAY OUT!

· There is no simple, magic cure. There are no synthetic drugs or substances that can pull you out. Methadone is not a cure.

· Hospitals can't help you on a permanent basis. Just ask anyone who has been there. Out of the hospital—right back to the spike. You can go back a hundred times and you would still be the same.

· No clinic can help you permanently—and deep in your heart you know it. Maybe you won't admit it, but it's true. How many times have you been to a clinic already? Right back to the stuff every time.

· No doctor, psychiatrist or hypnotist can cure you! A doctor can pacify you with some pills; a psychiatrist can tell you why you are an addict—but they cannot cure you!

· Cold turkey is the best and quickest way to start a cure. Cutting down on your supply with a medication is just an excuse to drag out your habit. Cold turkey never killed anybody. It's that way in jail—it's the best.

• *You must quit smoking! No addict can be permanently cured until he is off cigarettes for good. If you can't quit your little habits, how are you going to quit your big habits? Fufural is a toxin in tobacco that will drive you back to your needle! What's the difference if you are addicted to tobacco or drugs—they are both habits of the mind! I dare anyone in the world to prove to me an addict is really cured if he is still smoking!*

• *Don't ask for help just to please someone else. You are fooling yourself if you look for help just to keep a wife, mother or friend happy. You've got to want help yourself.*

• *You can't be cured in three weeks. So forget about a job and your future for a while. You have to get away from your so-called friends and from your connections. Out of the city, out of the community, out of the street. You don't need a job right now—you couldn't keep it anyway.*

• *Don't expect to be trusted or babied. You can't fool experienced people in the field of narcotics, so quit working angles. You may be sick—but you're not a little baby. If you can run around making connections, you can work for a cure. GET UP OFF YOUR SEAT AND QUIT ACTING LIKE A CRIPPLED BABY!*

STEP NUMBER THREE: GIVE YOURSELF OVER TO GOD!

• *God is the only one who can cure you! Nothing is impossible with God. If anyone claims cures outside of the power of God they are lying.*

• *You must come to Him like a little child and ask for help. He has never turned anyone down if they were sincere.*

• *You must believe that the Bible is the Word of God and that it has the secrets of your cure. You shall know the truth and the truth will make you free.*

• *It is not enough just to believe in God—you must believe in His Son, Jesus Christ. The Bible makes you this promise: If you will confess Jesus as your Saviour, He will make you into a new man. The old life will pass away and everything will become new!*

• *Open up your heart to God even more than you would to a psychiatrist and tell Him all about your problem. Then confess to Jesus all your sins and every bad thing you can remember you have done. Ask Him to forgive your sins and to come into your heart. He will drive out the desire for drugs and give you power over it!*

• *Don't just think your prayers to God—talk out loud to Him. While you are talking out loud to God you will suddenly know what prayer really is.*

• *Talk to God every day at least five times. Read the Bible every day and fill your mind with thoughts from its verses. Keep asking for His help—even if you have to do it a thousand times a day. He will never get tired of listening.*

• *You must have faith in God! When you connect with a pusher, how do you know he is not giving you rat poison instead of H? You shoot it up without testing it under a microscope because you must have faith it would be junk. If you can trust a pusher, why can't you trust in God—HE NEVER LETS YOU DOWN!*

STEP NUMBER FOUR: START PLANNING YOUR LIFE ALL OVER AGAIN!

• *The moment you surrender your life over to God—that is the time to start planning all over again. Think back to the time before you started on drugs. What was your ambition? Find what you want to do—then start making plans.*

- *All your plans must start with God. Make Him your partner and don't ever let Him leave your life. Don't make Him leave you by your neglect. Give God first chance to use your life. Maybe He will want you to help other addicts when you are fully cured.*
- *You can never again be around your old neighborhood or your old friends. Stay away from your old life as if it were hell itself. Don't go to your old hangouts just to test yourself to see if you are cured—that would be tempting God. Find new friends and brothers who are clean.*
- *If you had no plans for your life and if you are sure you can't help others, then mark down on a piece of paper FIVE things you think you would like to do or be. Spend a few weeks investigating what is involved in all of these five things, then choose the one that appeals to you most. You must choose a goal—you can never again be a loafer or a floater who has no ambition. KNOW WHAT YOU WANT TO DO—THEN GO AFTER IT! Indecision will ruin you.*
- *You must learn to love the things you once hated and learn to hate the things you once loved. You can do the right things now because God gives you power to do them.*

STEP NUMBER FIVE: SHAKE OFF ALL YOUR FEARS!

- *Fear is the demon that turned you into a drug addict to start with. When you turn your life over to God you never have to fear again. When Jesus comes to live in your heart, He drives away all fears and doubts.*
- *Don't be afraid you will go back to the needle! God guarantees a 100% cure. As long as you stay with God, He will stay with you. If you forsake God—you will go back. When He is with you—you need never fear.*
- *Don't be afraid of your past! When God forgives your sins—He forgets them. He will not hold them against you and He will make society forget them too. Make restitution when you can— but when you can't, leave it all in God's hand.*
- *Don't ever be afraid that God will drop you! He has never done that and He even promises to send an angel to watch over you in all your ways.*

· *Don't ever be afraid of what people will say or think! Keep your eyes on Jesus and you will never be disappointed or confused.*

· *When fear starts coming into your mind to confuse and bother you—when you start getting restless—get alone and kneel before God. Ask Him to keep your mind in perfect peace. HE WILL KEEP YOU FROM ALL YOUR FEARS!*

bible help for drug addicts

The Bible is never silent on any social problem. The Bible speaks loud and clear to all drug addicts. It exposes his heart—diagnoses his problem—pinpoints his predicament—offers a positive, lifetime solution—and motivates and prepares him for a new life. While the experts argue and the researchers punch the IBM cards with conflicting statistics and solutions, the Bible offers a sound, direct and simple answer that never changes.

The Bible refers to drugs and its usage as sorceries or witchcraft. This is taken from a Greek word *pharmakon* meaning drug.

There are over 200 Bible verses that deal directly with the addict and his problem. The *Teen Challenge Staff* has listed here only a few. These we call "THE SELF STARTER VERSES" and "BIBLE MOTIVATORS."

THE DRUG ADDICT'S PSALM (Psalm 31)

The following verses in particular:

<u>VERSE 4</u>: Pull me out of the net that they have laid privily for me: for thou art my strength.

<u>VERSE 9</u>: Have mercy upon me, O Lord, for I am in trouble: mine eye is consumed with grief, yea, my soul and my belly.

<u>VERSE 10</u>: For my life is spent with grief, and my years with sighing; my strength faileth because of mine iniquity, and my bones are consumed.

<u>VERSE 11</u>: I was a reproach among all mine enemies but especially among my neighbors, and a fear to mine acquaintance: they that did see me without fled from me.

THE DRUG ADDICT'S BLOOD

PSALM 9:12: When he maketh inquisition for blood, he remembereth them: he forgetteth not the cry of the humble.

PSALM 72:14: He shall redeem their souls from deceit and violence: AND PRECIOUS SHALL THEIR BLOOD BE IN HIS SIGHT.

THE DRUG ADDICT'S NEEDLE

PSALM 7:13: He hath also prepared for him THE INSTRUMENTS OF DEATH; he ordaineth his arrows against the persecutors.

THE DRUG ADDICT'S PROBLEM

PROVERBS 26:11: As a dog returneth to his vomit, so a FOOL RETURNETH TO HIS FOLLY (on drugs).

PROVERBS 5:22: His own iniquities shall take the wicked himself; AND HE SHALL BE HOLDEN WITH THE CORDS OF HIS SINS.

PSALM 10:4: The wicked, THROUGH THE PRIDE OF HIS COUNTENANCE, will not seek after God: God is not in all his thoughts.

DRUG ADDICTS FOOL THEMSELVES!

PSALM 10:6: He hath said in his heart, I shall not be moved: for I SHALL NEVER BE IN ADVERSITY.

PSALM 10:11: He hath said in his heart, GOD HATH FORGOTTEN: he hideth his face; HE WILL NEVER SEE IT.

PROVERBS 19:3: THE FOOLISHNESS OF MAN PERVERTETH HIS WAY: and his heart fretteth against the Lord.

PROVERBS 19:15: SLOTHFULNESS casteth into a deep sleep; and an IDLE SOUL shall suffer hunger.

PROVERBS 6:18: AN HEART THAT DEVISETH WICKED IMAGINATIONS, feet that be swift in running to mischief.

PSALM 73:14: For all the day long have I been plagued, and CHASTENED EVERY MORNING.

PSALM 69:2: I sink in DEEP MIRE, WHERE THERE IS NO STANDING: I am come into DEEP WATERS, where the FLOODS overflow me.

PROVERBS 26:12: Seest thou A MAN WISE IN HIS OWN CONCEIT? There is more hope of a fool than of him.

PROVERBS 28:13: He that covereth his sins shall not prosper: but whoso CONFESSETH AND FORSAKETH them shall have mercy.

PROVERBS 29:1: He, that BEING OFTEN REPROVED HARDENETH HIS NECK, shall suddenly be destroyed, and that without remedy.

PSALM 77:2: In the day of my trouble I sought the Lord: MY SORE RAN IN THE NIGHT, AND CEASED NOT: my soul refused to be comforted.

THE DRUG ADDICT'S PRAYER

PSALM 69:5: O God, THOU KNOWEST MY FOOLISH-NESS: and my sins are not hid from thee.

PSALM 44:15: My CONFUSION is continually before me, and the SHAME of my face hath covered me.

PSALM 51:9: Hide thy face from my sins, and BLOT OUT ALL MINE INIQUITIES.

PSALM 35:10: All my bones shall say, Lord, who is like unto thee, WHICH DELIVEREST THE POOR FROM HIM THAT IS TOO STRONG FOR HIM, yea, the poor and the needy from him that SPOILETH him?

PSALM 55:23: But thou, O God, shall bring them down into the pit of destruction: BLOODY AND DECEITFUL MEN SHALL NOT LIVE OUT HALF THEIR DAYS; but I will trust in thee.

PSALM 56:9: When I cry unto thee, THEN SHALL MINE ENEMIES TURN BACK; this I know; for God is for me.

PSALM 56:10: In God will I praise his word: in the Lord will I PRAISE HIS WORD.

PSALM 56:11: In God have I put my trust: I WILL NOT BE AFRAID WHAT MAN CAN DO UNTO ME.

PSALM 56:13: For thou hast DELIVERED MY SOUL FROM DEATH: wilt not thou DELIVER MY FEET FROM FALLING, that I may walk before God in the LIGHT of the living?

PSALM 34:6: THIS POOR MAN CRIED, AND THE LORD HEARD HIM, AND SAVED HIM OUT OF ALL HIS TROUBLES.

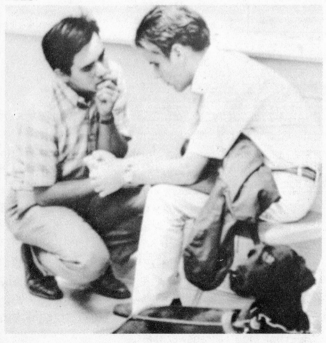

PSALM 49:15: But GOD WILL REDEEM MY SOUL FROM THE POWER OF THE GRAVE: for he shall receive me. Selah.

PSALM 55:18: He hath delivered my soul in peace from the battle that was against me: FOR THERE WERE MANY WITH ME.

PSALM 71:1: In thee, O Lord, do I put my trust: LET ME NEVER BE PUT TO CONFUSION.

PSALM 69:17: And hide not thy face from thy servant;

FOR I AM IN TROUBLE: hear me speedily.

PSALM 34:4: I sought the Lord, and he heard me, and DELIVERED ME FROM ALL MY FEARS.

PSALM 73:24: Thou shalt GUIDE ME WITH THY COUNSEL, and afterward receive me to glory.

PSALM 73:26: My flesh and my heart faileth: but GOD IS THE STRENGTH OF MY HEART, and my portion for ever.

PSALM 77:1: I CRIED unto God WITH MY VOICE, even unto God with my voice; and he gave ear unto me.

PSALM 71:20: Thou, which hast shewed me great and SORE TROUBLES, shalt quicken me again, and SHALT BRING ME UP AGAIN from the depths of the earth.

PSALM 71:2: Deliver me in thy righteousness, and CAUSE ME TO ESCAPE: incline thine ear unto me, and save me.

PSALM 71:3: Be thou my strong habitation, WHEREUNTO I MAY CONTINUALLY RESORT: thou hast given commandment to save me; for thou art my rock and my fortress.

PSALM 86:7: In the day of my trouble I WILL CALL UPON THEE: for thou wilt answer me.

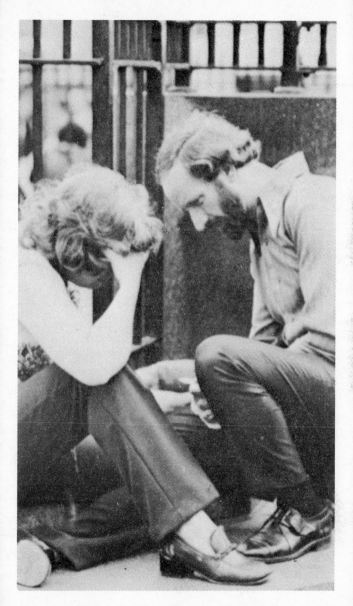

PSALM 108:12: Give us help from trouble: FOR VAIN IS THE HELP OF MAN.

Psalm 116:6: The Lord PRESERVETH the simple: I WAS BROUGHT LOW, and he helped me.

PSALM 116:8: FOR THOU HAST DELIVERED MY SOUL FROM DEATH, MINE EYES FROM TEARS, AND MY FEET FROM FALLING.

PSALM 119:45: And I will walk at LIBERTY: for I seek thy precepts.

PSALM 118:6: The Lord is on my side; I will not fear: WHAT CAN MAN DO UNTO ME?

PSALM 118:8: It is better to TRUST IN THE LORD than to put confidence in man.

PSALM 118:17: I SHALL NOT DIE, BUT LIVE, and declare the works of the Lord.

PSALM 119:9 WHEREWITHAL SHALL A YOUNG MAN CLEANSE HIS WAY? by taking heed thereto according to thy word.

PSALM 119:11: Thy word have I hid IN MINE HEART, that I might not sin against thee.

PSALM 119:29: REMOVE FROM ME THE WAY OF LYING: and grant me thy law graciously.

PSALM 86:15: But thou, O Lord, art a God FULL OF COMPASSION, and gracious, LONGSUFFERING and plenteous in mercy and truth.

PSALM 50:15: CALL upon me in the day of trouble: I WILL DELIVER THEE, and thou shalt glorify me.

PROVERBS 19:23: The fear of the Lord tendeth to life: and he that hath it shall ABIDE SATISFIED; HE SHALL NOT BE VISITED WITH EVIL.

why kids take drugs

Teenagers use drugs for a variety of reasons. Among them are:

1. As a symbol of independence and a slap at society for its failures.

2. To escape unhappy home situations, including phony, cruel dads and pill-intoxicated moms.

3. Curiosity—to find out what everybody's talking about.

4. To be accepted by a group that is hip.

5. Gang and group influences that make risks seem small.

6. To escape from problems, such as boy and girlfriend troubles, school worries, inability to make friends.

7. Fear of being chicken—a willingness to accept a dare and try anything once.

8. Because it's illegal—providing a sense of belonging to the NOW generation of rebellion and self-assertion.

9. Misinformation or self-persuasion based on slanted research and firsthand testimony from friends who claimed to have enjoyed their ''trips.''

10. The challenge of going to the brink of insanity. It's a game of mind bending to ''test your head.''

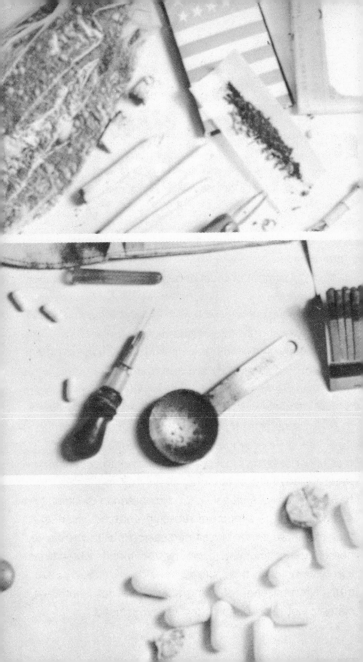

how to recognize drugs

1. MARIJUANA cannot be confused with tobacco. It is green rather than brown and smells sweet like alfalfa when burning. The sticks are rolled in straw paper and tucked in the ends—rolled shut to prevent loss of the weed. The tips burn brightly when first lit. Marijuana joints do not look like factory manufactured cigarettes.

2. HEROIN is sold in small glassine bags, or in capsules. The powder is white and has an extremely bitter taste in its pure state. When mixed with milk sugar (lactose), it is sweet. The small bags are about the size of a postage stamp.

3. PILLS (amphetamines and barbiturates) are available in capsule and tablet form in various pastel colors. The combination of amphetamines and barbiturates is sold in triangular shapes. No pill should be taken without positive identification. Pills produced by legitimate companies often have various markings and are more easily identified.

4. ACID There are no standard dosage forms or markings that make visual identification possible. LSD comes in homemade capsules or tablets, sometimes in powder or liquid form. LSD can be impregnated in sugar cubes, chewing gum, candy, ink blotters, crackers, postage stamps, aspirins, vitamins and handkerchiefs.

how to get information

1. American Medical Association
   Department of Mental Health
   535 North Dearborn Street
   Chicago, Illinois 60610

(Ask for list of selected reading material on drug abuse and drug dependence)

2. Narcotics Education, Inc.
   Box 4390
   6830 Laurel Street, N.W.
   Washington, D.C. 20012

(Ask for list of brochures on drugs. I recommend these people as among the best)

3. U.S. Department of Health, Education and Welfare
   Superintendent of Documents
   U.S. Government Printing Office
   Washington, D.C. 20402

(Ask for list of pamphlets on narcotics)

4. *Regional Offices* – Bureau of Narcotics and Dangerous Drugs

ATLANTA
1831 Peachtree Road, N.E.
Atlanta, Georgia 30309

BALTIMORE
401 Water Street
Baltimore, Maryland 21220

BOSTON
J.F. Kennedy Federal Building
Suite E-311
Boston, Massachusetts 02203

CHICAGO
Suite 1700, Engineering Bldg.
205 West Wacker Drive
Chicago, Illinois 60606

DALLAS
1114 Commerce Street
Dallas, Texas 75202

DENVER
228 New Customs House
712 - 19th Street
Denver, Colorado 80202

DETROIT
602 Federal Bldg. & Courthouse
231 W. Lafayette
Detroit, Michigan 48226

LOS ANGELES
714 W. Olympic Blvd.
Room 1010
Los Angeles, California 90015

MINNEAPOLIS
402 Federal Building
110 South Fourth Street
Minneapolis, Minnesota 55401

NEW YORK
201 Varick Street
New York, New York 10014

PHILADELPHIA
605 U.S. Custom House
Second and Chestnut Streets
Philadelphia, Pennsylvania 19106

SAN FRANCISCO
450 Golden Gate Avenue
Room 2041
San Francisco, California 94102

SEATTLE
Immigrant Station
311 U.S. Courthouse
Seattle, Washington 98134

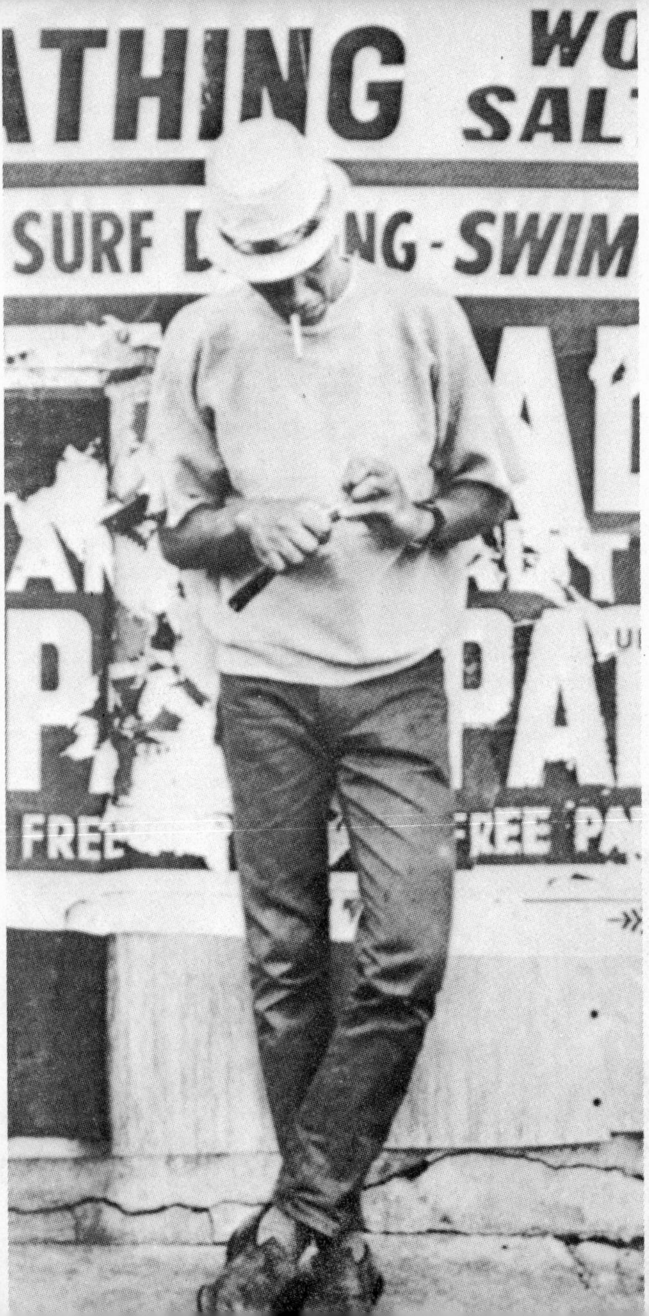
ATHING
WO
SALT
SURF
NG-SWIM
FREE
FREE PA

glossary

ACID	LSD 25
ACID HEAD	LSD user
BAG	A container of drugs
BALLOON	Rubber toy balloon used for storing or delivering narcotics, usually capped heroin
BARBS	Barbiturates
BENNIES	Amphetamines (benzedrine)
BINDLE	A container of drugs
BLAST	To smoke a marijuana cigarette
BLOW	To smoke a marijuana cigarette
BLOWN MIND	Extreme hallucination
BLUE BANDS	Carbrital (Pentobarbital Sodium-Carbromal)
BLUE BIRDS	Amytal (Amobarbital Sodium)
BLUE CHEER	Type of LSD
BLUE DEVILS	Amytal (Amobarbital Sodium)
BLUE HEAVEN	Amytal (Amobarbital Sodium)
BLUES	Amytal (Amobarbital Sodium)
BOMBED	Intoxicated on drugs
BOOSTER	Consumption or injection of additional dosage to continue or prolong a "trip"
BREAD	Money
BRICK	Kilo of marijuana in compressed brick form
BRIDGE	See "CRUTCH"—usually alligator clamp or like device used to hold marijuana cigarette while smoking same

BUMMER	A bad trip
BURN	To buy phony drugs or to burn the skin when injecting
BUTTON	Peyote buttons
CAN	One ounce of marijuana. Term used from tobacco can in which marijuana was commonly sold in the past. Now it is more frequently sold in small paper bags.
CANDY	Barbiturates
CAP	Capsule containing a drug
CARGA	Load or supply of narcotics or drugs
CARRYING	In possession of a drug
CARTWHEEL	Amphetamine tablet (round, white double-scored)
CHICKEN POWDER	Amphetamine powder for injection
CHIPPY	An occasional user of heroin
CHIVA	Heroin
CHRISTMAS TREE	Tuinal
CLEAN	Removing stems and seeds from marijuana. Also, addict who is free from narcotic injection marks, as in "I'm clean, man."
COKE	Cocaine
COLD TURKEY	Breaking the habit of drug use at home, in prison, etc., without the aid of any medication or medical care
COME DOWN	To come off from drugs
CONNECT	To buy drugs
CONNECTION	A peddler who knows an addict and will sell him drugs
COOKER	Bottle cap for heating drug powder with water
COP	To purchase drugs
CO-PILOTS	Amphetamines
COTTONS	Bits of cotton saturated with narcotic solution used to strain foreign matter when drawing solution up into hypodermic syringe or eyedropper. These "cottons" are often saved by addicts for an emergency, as they contain a residual amount of the drug.
CRASH PAD	Temporary residence, usually for a night or two, usually communal
CRUTCH	Device used to hold marijuana cigarette when it has burned to the point where it will burn the fingers. Also container for hypodermic needle
CRYSTALS	Amphetamine powder for injection
CUBE 8	Sugar cube impregnated with LSD

CUT	To dilute a powder with milk sugar, baking powder, etc.
"D"	LSD
DEALER	Drug supplier
DECK	A small packet of morphine, cocaine, or heroin
DET	Diethyltryptamine
DEXIES	Amphetamine tablets
DMT	Diethyltryptamine
DOPE	Any narcotic
DOTTING	Placing LSD on a sugar cube
DOWNER	To come off from drugs. Also, a depressant type drug such as a barbiturate
DEUCE BAG	A two-dollar container of a drug
FAT	Describing someone who has a good supply of drugs
FIT	Equipment for injecting drugs
FIX	To inject drugs or one dose of a particular drug; also "OUTFIT"
FLASH	Initial high feeling when injecting amphetamines and other drugs
FLUSH	The initial feeling the user gets when injecting methamphetamine
FOOTBALLS	Amphetamine tablets (oval shaped)
FREAK	A person who injects amphetamines
FREAK OUT	To have a drug party
FUZZ	The law
GARBAGE	Poor quality drugs
GEEZE	Injection of narcotic
GOURD	Head
GOOD H	A good quality of heroin
GOOFER	One who drops pills
GOOFED UP	Under the influence of barbiturates
GRAM	Gram of heroin (approximately 10 capsules)
GRASS	Marijuana
GRASSHOPPER	Marijuana user
H.	Heroin
HABIT	Physically or psychologically dependent on drugs
HASH	Hashish
HEAD	An LSD user
HEARTS	Dexedrine (orange-colored, heart-shaped tablets)
HEAT	A police officer—the law
HEAVY	Heroin
HIGH	A drug user who is "up" or under the influence of a drug, usually a stimulant

HIT	One dose of a particular drug
HOG	An addict who uses all he can get his hands on
HOOKED	Addicted; a confirmed addict
HORNING	Sniffing narcotics through nasal passages
HYPE	A person who takes drugs by injection
HYPE OUTFIT	Equipment for injecting drugs
IT-290	Hallucinogen, alpha-methyl tryptamine
J or JAY	Joint or marijuana cigarette
JAR DEALER	A person who sells drugs in 1,000 tablet or capsule bottles
JOINT	A marijuana cigarette; also State Prison
JOLT	An injection of narcotics
JOY POPPING	Irregular drug habit
JUG	1,000 tablet or capsule bottle
JUNK	Heroin
K-2	Type of LSD
KEE	Kilo
KEG	25,000 amphetamine capsules or tablets, or more
KICK	To stop using drugs (See "COLD TURKEY")
KILO	2.2 pounds
"L"	LSD
LAB	Equipment used to manufacture drugs illegally
LAID OUT	Being informed on
LOADED	High on drugs
MAINLINER	One who injects directly into a vein
MAN	A drug supplier or a police officer
MANICURE	Prepare marijuana for use in cigarettes
MARY JANE	Marijuana
MED	Hallucinogen, methyl-3, 4-methylenedioxy-phenethylamine
METH	Amphetamine Powder (Methamphetamine Hydrocholoride)
MELLOW YELLOWS	Pale yellow LSD powder or cigarettes made from banana peel scrapings
MICKEY	Chloral Hydrate
MICKEY FINN	Chloral Hydrate
MIND BLOWER	Pure, unadulterated drugs
MOTA	Marijuana
NARK	Narcotics agents
NEEDLE	Hypodermic needle
NICKEL BUY	A $5.00 purchase
O.D.	Overdose – usually death
OUTFIT	Equipment for injection by the hypodermic method; a "hype" outfit. Eyedropper and needle, spoon, safety pin, etc.

OZ-OUNCE	Refers to ounce of narcotics, usually heroin or meth. Same as "PIECE"
PANIC	When a drug supply has been cut off
PAPER	A container of drugs
P.C.P. H	Hallucinogenic substance Sernylan (Phencyclidine HCL)
PEACE PILL	Hallucinogenic substance Sernylan (Phencyclidine HCL)
PER	A prescription
PEZ	PEZ candies impregnated with LSD
PIECE	One ounce of heroin
PILL HEAD	Amphetamine or barbiturate user
POINT	Hypodermic needle
POP	A subcutaneous injection, usually referred to as "skin popping"
POPPER	Amyl Nitrate in ampule form, inhaled immediately after taking LSD
POT	Marijuana
POWDER	Amphetamine Powder
PUSHER	Drug peddler to users. One who seeks more business from regular customers
QUARTER	Quarter of an ounce of either heroin or meth, usually 4 to 8 grams
QUARTER DECK	¼ of a deck—paper containing heroin or amphetamine
RAINBOWS	Tuinal (Amobarbital Sodium and Secobarbital Sodium)
REDS	Seconal (Secobarbital Sodium)
REDS AND BLUES	Tuinal (Amobarbital Sodium and Secobarbital Sodium)
RED BIRDS	Seconal (Secobarbital Sodium)
RED DEVILS	Seconal (Secobarbital Sodium)
REEFER	Marijuana cigarette
ROACH	Small butt of marijuana cigarette
ROLL	A tin foil wrapped roll of tablets
ROLL DEALER	A person who sells tablets in rolls
RUN	To take drugs continuously for at least 3 days
SCORE	Make a drug purchase
SCRIPT	Drug prescription
SHOOTING GALLERY	Place where users can purchase drugs and inject them
SHOOT UP	To inject drugs
SKIN POPPING	Intradermal or subcutaneous injection
SLEEPERS	A depressant type drug such as barbiturates
SMACK	Drugs, especially powdered drugs in the form of snuff

SNIFFING	Using narcotics by sniffing through nasal passages, usually heroin or cocaine
SNITCH	Informer, stoolie
SNOW	LSD Powder, Amphetamine Powder, or Cocaine
SNOWBIRD	Cocaine user
SOURCE	Supplier of drugs or narcotics
SPATZ	Capsules
SPEED	Amphetamine powder for injection
SPEEDBALL	A powerful shot of drug, usually heroin and cocaine combined
SPIKE	Hypodermic needle
SPOON	A measure for a drug in powder form. 16 spoons per ounce
STASH	Place where narcotic or the ''outfit'' is hidden
STONED	Under the influence of drugs
STP	4-methyl 2, 5 Dimethoxy Alpha Methyl Phenethylamine
STRAIGHT	Under the influence of narcotics
STRUNG OUT	Heavily addicted
STUFF	General term for drugs and narcotics
SYNDICATE ACID	STP
TASTE	A small quantity of drugs or narcotics—a sample
TD CAPS	Time disintegrating capsules
TEA	Marijuana
TOKE UP	To light a marijuana cigarette
TRACKS	A series of puncture wounds in the veins, caused by continued narcotic injections
TREY	A $3.00 purchase
TRICK	An easy mark, sucker, patsy
TRIGGER	To smoke a marijuana cigarette immediately after taking LSD
TRIP	The hallucinations and/or feelings experienced by a person after taking a drug
TURN ON	To take a drug
UP TIGHT	Angry
USER	One who uses narcotics
WASTED	High or drunk
WEDGES	Small tables made from tablet board
WEED	Marijuana
WEED HEAD	Marijuana smoker
WEEKEND HABIT	Irregular habit
WEST COAST	Amphetamine Tablets or Capsules
WHITES	Amphetamine Tablets
WORKS	Equipment for injecting drugs
YELLOW JACKETS	Nembutal (Pentobarbital Sodium)
YELLOWS	Nembutal (Pentobarbital Sodium)

GOD'S WORD PROMISES VICTORY!

- But the Lord is faithful, and He will strengthen and protect you from the evil one. II Thessalonians 3:3

- My Father, who has given them to Me, is greater than all; and no one is able to snatch them out of the Father's hand. John 10:29

- He which establisheth us with you in Christ, and hath anointed us, is God. II Corinthians 1:21

- Being confident of this very thing, that he which hath begun a good work in you will perform it until the day of Jesus Christ. Philippians 1:6

- I am persuaded, that neither death, nor life, nor angels, nor principalities, nor powers, nor things present, nor things to come, nor height, nor depth, nor any other creature, shall be able to separate us from the love of God, which is in Christ Jesus our Lord. Romans 8:38,39

- Who are kept by the power of God through faith unto salvation. I Peter 1:5

- Unto Him that is able to keep you from falling, and to present you faultless before the presence of his glory with exceeding joy. Jude 24

- Give diligence to make your calling and election sure: for if ye do these things, ye shall never fall. II Peter 1:10

- No one who has become part of God's family makes a practice of sinning, for Christ, God's Son, holds him securely and the devil cannot get his hands on him. I John 5:18

- God Himself shall be with them, and be their God. Revelation 21:3

- He shall feed his flock like a shepherd: he shall gather the lambs with his arm, and carry them in his bosom, and shall gently lead those that are with young. Isaiah 40:11

- Though I walk in the midst of trouble, thou wilt revive me: thou shalt stretch forth thine hand against the wrath of mine enemies, and thy right hand shall save me. Psalm 138:7

- Holy Father, keep through thine own name those whom thou hast given me. John 17:11

- The Lord shall be thy confidence, and shall keep thy foot from being taken. Proverbs 3:26

- The angel of the Lord encampeth round about them that fear him, and delivereth them. Psalm 34:7

- I have set the Lord always before me; because he is at my right hand, I shall not be moved. Psalm 16:8

- Behold, he that keepeth Israel shall neither slumber nor sleep. The Lord is thy keeper. Psalm 121:4,5

- Thou art my hiding place; thou shalt preserve me from trouble; thou shalt compass me about with songs of deliverance. Psalm 32:7

- God will redeem my soul from the power of the grave: for he shall receive me. Psalm 49:15

- If the Spirit of Him who raised Jesus from the dead dwells in you, He who raised Christ Jesus from the dead will also give life to your mortal bodies through His Spirit who indwells you. Romans 8:11

- The blood of Christ, who through the eternal spirit offered himself without spot to God, purged your conscience from dead works to serve the living God. Hebrews 9:14

- But now in Christ Jesus you who formerly were far off have been brought near by the blood of Christ. Ephesians 2:13

- Knowing that you were not redeemed with perishable things like silver or gold from your futile way of life inherited from your forefathers, but with precious blood, as of a lamb unblemished and spotless, the blood of Christ. I Peter 1:18, 19

- And since by his blood he did all this for us as sinners, how much more will he do for us now that he has declared us not guilty? Now he will save us from all of God's wrath to come. Romans 5:9

- For Christ's death on the cross has made peace with God for all by his blood. Colossians 1:20

GOD PROMISES MIRACLES!

- For I can do everything God asks me to with the help of Christ who gives me the strength and power. Philippians 4:13

- Not that we are sufficient of ourselves to think anything as of ourselves; but our sufficiency is of God. II Corinthians 3:5

- Now unto him that is able to do exceeding abundantly above all that we ask or think, according to the power that worketh in us. Esphesians 3:20

- If two of you shall agree on earth as touching any thing that they shall ask, it shall be done for them of my Father which is in heaven. Matthew 18:19

- If thou canst believe, all things are possible to him that believeth, Mark 9:23

- Verily, verily, I say unto you, He that believeth on me, the works that I do shall he do also; and greater works than these shall he do; because I go unto my Father. John 14:12

- Fear thou not; for I am with thee: be not dismayed; for I am thy God: I will strengthen thee; yea, I will uphold thee with the right hand of my righteousness. Isaiah 41:10

- My covenant will I not break, nor alter the thing that is gone out of my lips. Psalm 89:34

- For the Lord God is a sun and shield: the Lord will give grace and glory; no good thing will he withhold from them that walk uprightly. Psalm 84:11

- Then shalt thou call, and the Lord shall answer; thou shalt cry, and he shall say, Here I am. Isaiah 58:9

- In whom we have boldness and access with confidence by the faith of him. Ephesians 3:12

- Seek not ye what ye shall eat, or what ye shall drink, neither be ye of doubtful mind. But rather seek ye the kingdom of God; and all these things shall be added unto you. Luke 12:29, 31

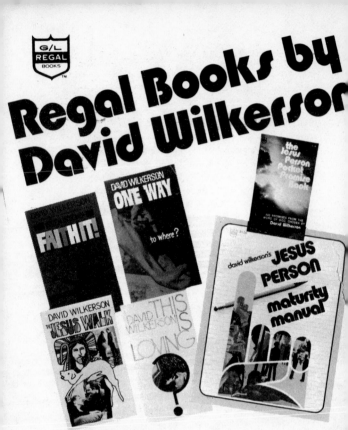